ANCIENT HISTORY AT A GLANCE

ANCIENT HISTORY
AT A GLANCE

How the Bible Connects History

LOIS CLYMER

Ancient History at a Glance, How the Bible Connects History

Copyright © Lois Clymer.

All rights reserved. No part of this publication may be reproduced, stored, or transmitted in any form or by any means, electronic, mechanical, photocopying, recording, scanning, or otherwise without written permission from the author. It is illegal to copy this book, post it to a website, or distribute it by any other means without permission.

Unless otherwise noted, scripture quotations are taken from the New American Standard Bible (NASB), Copyright © 1960, 1962, 1963, 1968, 1971, 1972, 1973, 1975, 1977, 1995, by the Lockman Foundation. www.Lockman.org.

Printed in the USA

2022 – First Edition

ISBN: 978-0-578-37640-0

Acknowledgment

My deep appreciation goes to Ethan, Amelia, Emma, Abigail, Clara, Cassedy, Stella, Shiloh, Lyv, and Layne, whose drawings and photos helped to illustrate this book.

Photo by Ethan

Contents

Introduction 1

Chapter 1: Finding Written and Recorded History 3

Chapter 2: Following the Ancestry of Jesus Christ 6

Chapter 3: Timeline of Patriarchs..8

Chapter 4: The Timeline Adds the Fourth Patriarch 10

Chapter 5: Father of Those Who Live in Tents..........................12

Chapter 6: Father of Those Who Play the Harp and Flute 14

Chapter 7: A Forger of Bronze and Iron....................................16

Chapter 8: Methuselah, the Eighth Patriarch 18

Chapter 9: Early Writing..20

Chapter 10: Noah, the Tenth Patriarch......................................23

Chapter 11: Enoch, An Eminent Astronomer 25

Chapter 12: The First Astronomers..27

Chapter 13: Long Lives of The Patriarchs.................................29

Chapter 14: A Mathematical Decay Curve 31

Chapter 15: Wickedness of Man Brings Flood..........................33

Chapter 16: Family of Noah Saved 34

Chapter 17: The Promise of the Rainbow 36

Chapter 18:	Kingdom of Nimrod	37
Chapter 19:	First Generations after The Great Flood	39
Chapter 20:	Egypt and its Pyramids	41
Chapter 21:	Empire of Sargon	43
Chapter 22:	The Minoans	45
Chapter 23:	Empire of Hammurabi	47
Chapter 24:	Family of Jacob (Israel)	49
Chapter 25:	The Hittite Empire	51
Chapter 26:	Moses Leads Israelites Out of Egypt	53
Chapter 27:	The Mycenae People	55
Chapter 28:	City of Troy Destroyed	57
Chapter 29:	The Phoenicians	59
Chapter 30:	The Israelites	61
Chapter 31:	King Solomon of Israel	63
Chapter 32:	The Celts	65
Chapter 33:	Fall of Israel	67
Chapter 34:	Assyrian Empire	69
Chapter 35:	Babylonian Empire	71
Chapter 36:	Persian Empire	73
Chapter 37:	Persians Attack Greece	75
Chapter 38:	Alexander the Great	77
Chapter 39:	The Punic Wars	79
Chapter 40:	The Roman Empire	81

About the Author 83

Introduction

What can we learn from written history? Where do we find written history? We have ancient historians such as Herodotus, sometimes called the father of history, and many others who lived after him. Herodotus lived 484–425 BC. History before that time can be difficult to find. Sometimes, lists of kings were written on temple walls, but they were difficult to date and verify.

Archaeologists who have uncovered ancient cities have unearthed many cuneiform tablets that they date to 3000 BC or earlier. These tablets reveal bits and pieces of history.

We also have a history of the Israelites and neighboring peoples in the Old Testament of the Bible.

What can we learn from history? It seems people were much the same as they are today. They built houses and cities and raised animals and vegetables for food. We read of powerful leaders and many wars, just as we have had in recent times.

The Bible has always been of particular interest to archeologists and academic historians because of its continuous thread, which is rare. In this book, I have created a timeline of written history, using the genealogy of Jesus Christ found in Luke, Chapter 3, of the Bible, which, by counting backward, comes to about 4000 BC. We have relatively little information regarding the first 1500 years or so, but after that, written history picks up, both with the history found in the Bible and with modern accounts. We find powerful rulers who formed empires, such as Sargon, who united the city states of Akkad and Sumer, possibly forming the first empire. Then we find more empires in that region. First came the Babylonian Empire of King Hammurabi, who created a short-lived empire, and then, the Assyrian empire, which was followed by the Second Babylonian Empire. After the fall of that empire, the Persians in the East built their empire, and later, Alexander the Great from Macedonia, north of Greece, built a huge empire. Finally, as the BC era comes to an end, the Romans continued to extend their vast and long-lasting empire.

I have tried to choose events and other bits and pieces of information that give us a snapshot of ancient history. Some of my grandchildren, ages six to twenty-one, helped me to illustrate this book. Enjoy the drawings and photos. May this panorama give you a glimpse of our ancient past.

CHAPTER 1

Finding Written and Recorded History

WRITTEN AND RECORDED HISTORY

We have much history written by various historians such as the Greek Herodotus, Thucydides from Athens, Eusebius of Caesarea, the Egyptian priest Manetho, Josephus of Jerusalem, and others. It is difficult, however, to put all the events they write about into a timeline. Historians struggle to count the years back from known events to piece together a chronology. Therefore, dates seem to be always changing as new writings are discovered and the picture becomes more complete.

THE GENEALOGIES OF JESUS CHRIST

One source that is fairly easy to trace is the Bible's genealogy of Jesus Christ. This timeline contains details that can be meshed with other known events. In the New Testament book of Luke, we find a list of all the ancestors of Jesus: He was the son, so it was thought, of Joseph, the son of Eli (Luke 3:23). What follows is a list of seventy-five names, beginning with Joseph and ending with "Adam, the son of God."

In ancient times, in many places, it was important to people to keep track of their ancestors. The Jews kept meticulous records of their ancestors.

Using this list and counting backward, we come to approximately 4000 BC for the beginning of Jesus Christ's ancestry. The Bible is the story of Jesus Christ. Genesis, the first book, promises that a redeemer will come, who will reverse the curse of sin and death. God selects a people through whom Christ will come (Israelites). There are many prophecies regarding his coming.

ADAM, THE FIRST MAN

We are told in Genesis that "In the beginning, God created the heavens and the earth." He placed the first man, Adam, and the first woman, Eve, in a beautiful garden in Eden.

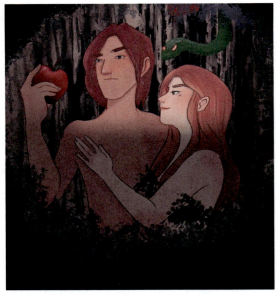

Drawing by Cassedy

When Adam and Eve ate the forbidden fruit (disobeyed God), they were put out of the garden, and would die someday. But at that time, God promised a redeemer ("the seed of the woman," Genesis 3:15) who would restore what they had lost: he would defeat death.

GOD MADE ALL THE ANIMALS

Drawings by Layne

CHAPTER 2

Following the Ancestry of Jesus Christ

The Bible has an interesting way of creating a timeline by stating the age of the father when a son was born. So, we are told in Genesis 5:3 that Adam, at the age of 130 years, had a son named Seth.

TIMELINE OF THE FIRST TWO PATRIARCHS

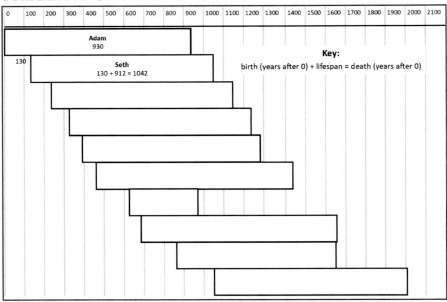

3900 BC

PROFILE OF AN ANCIENT HISTORIAN

Herodotus was called the father of history by the Roman scholar Cicero. He lived in Greece around 484–425 BC. He was one of the first writers to do a systematic investigation of historical events. He wrote *The Histories*, a detailed account of the Greco-Persian wars. Look for information on the Greco-Persian Wars in Chapter 37.

He is a leading source of information not only for Greece 550–479 BC but also for much of western Asia and Egypt at that time. He is considered the father of history because he is the first person to write what we would consider real history, meaning that he used his own knowledge and the testimony of others to attempt a systematic writing of past events.

CHAPTER 3

Timeline of Patriarchs

TRACING THE ANCESTRY OF JESUS CHRIST

Starting at the beginning, we have Adam and Seth. Next comes Enosh. Seth, at the age of 105 years, had a son named Enosh (Genesis 5:6).

TIMELINE OF THE FIRST THREE PATRIARCHS

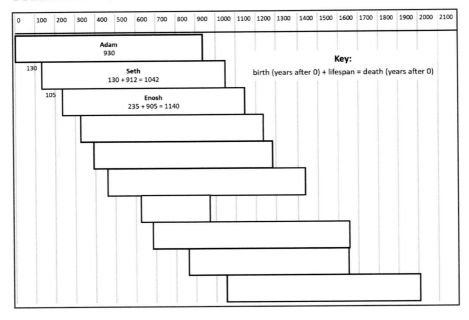

3800 BC

PROFILE OF A HISTORIAN

Thucydides was born around 460 BC and was a contemporary of Herodotus. He complained that Herodotus made up stories to make his history lectures more interesting, while he himself, he claimed, used strict standards of impartiality and evidence gathering. Thucydides wrote the *History of the Peloponnese War*. That war was fought in Greece between Athens and Sparta.

CHAPTER 4

The Timeline Adds the Fourth Patriarch

TRACING THE ANCESTRY OF JESUS CHRIST

Enosh, at the age of ninety years, had a son named Kenan (Genesis 5:9). Starting with Adam, we had Seth, Enosh, and now Kenan.

TIMELINE OF THE FIRST FOUR PATRIARCHS.

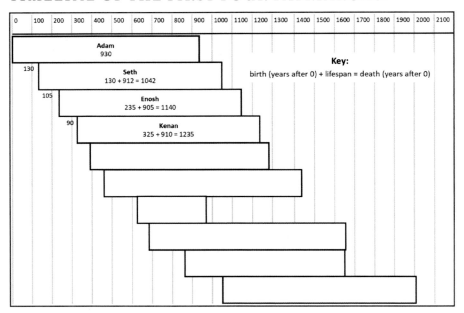

3700 BC

PROFILE OF AN ANCIENT HISTORIAN

Xenophon of Athens lived around 430–354 BC and is described as a military leader, philosopher, and historian. As an excellent military strategist, he outlined the military and political methods of Cyrus the Great. We meet with Cyrus the Great in Chapter 36. Regarding Xenophon, the military historian Theodore Dodge wrote, "The centuries since have devised nothing to surpass the genius of this warrior." He established precedents for many logistic operations and was a student and friend of Socrates.

Xenophon, iStock.com

CHAPTER 5

Father of Those Who Live in Tents

FATHER OF THOSE WHO LIVE IN TENTS AND HAVE LIVESTOCK

Around this time lived Jabal, who was the father of people who live in tents and raise livestock (Genesis 4:20).

LIVING IN TENTS

Drawing by Emma

3600 BC

TRACING THE ANCESTRY OF JESUS CHRIST

Kenan, at the age of seventy, had a son named Mahalalel (Genesis 5:12). For the earliest patriarchs we now have Adam, Seth, Enosh, Kenan, Mahalalel.

TIMELINE OF THE FIRST FIVE PATRIARCHS

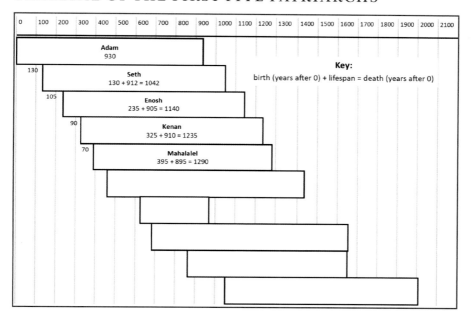

CHAPTER 6

Father of Those Who Play the Harp and Flute

FATHER OF ALL THOSE WHO PLAY THE HARP AND FLUTE

Jabal, the father of those who live in tents, had a brother whose name was Jubal. He was the father of all those who play the harp and flute (Genesis 4:21).

TRACING THE ANCESTRY OF JESUS CHRIST

Mahalalel, at the age of sixty-five, had a son named Jared (Genesis 5:15). We have now covered the last six names in Luke 3:37–38: "the son of Jared, the son of Mahalalel, the son of Kenan (Cainan), the son of Enosh, the son of Seth, the son of Adam, the son of God."

HARP
Drawing by Shiloh

3500 BC

TIMELINE OF THE FIRST SIX PATRIARCHS

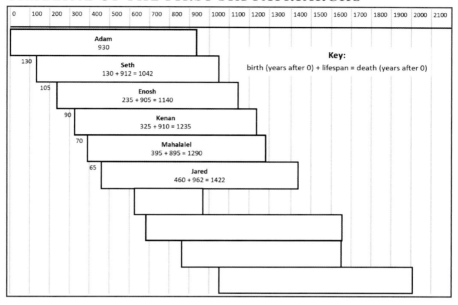

Key:
birth (years after 0) + lifespan = death (years after 0)

CHAPTER 7

A Forger of Bronze and Iron

FATHER OF INSTRUMENTS OF BRONZE AND IRON

Another brother of Jabal and Jubal was Tubal-cain. He was a forger of all instruments of bronze and iron (Genesis 4:22).

HAMMER FOR FORGING

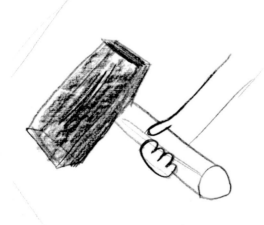

Drawing by Clara

3400 BC

TRACING THE ANCESTRY OF JESUS CHRIST

Jared, at the age of 162, had a son named Enoch (Genesis 5:18).

TIMELINE OF THE FIRST SEVEN PATRIARCHS

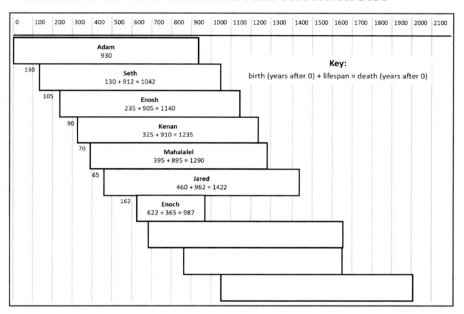

CHAPTER 8

Methuselah, the Eighth Patriarch

TRACING THE ANCESTRY OF JESUS CHRIST

Enoch at the age of sixty-five had a son named Methuselah (Genesis 5:21). We now have eight entries on our patriarchs timeline (see below).

TIMELINE OF THE FIRST EIGHT PATRIARCHS

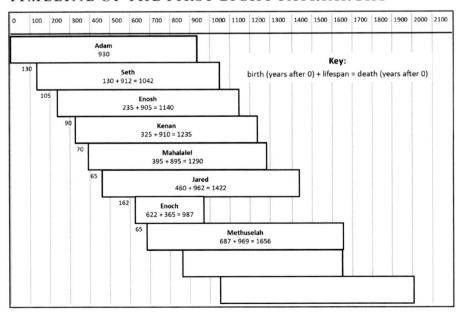

3300 BC

PROFILE OF AN ANCIENT HISTORIAN

Manetho was an Egyptian priest who moved to Greece and wrote exclusively in Greek. Born around 323 BC, he wrote about Egyptian dynasties. His division of rulers into dynasties was his innovation. He did not use this term to refer to bloodlines, but instead, inserted a new dynasty wherever he detected some kind of discontinuity.

Unfortunately, no copies of his complete original works have survived, but some sections have been quoted by other writers. The many existing versions differ, and variations in spelling and reign length are common. Many historians throughout the years have tried to put together the Egyptian history.

Manetho's Egyptian history became involved in a rivalry among historians and disputes arose concerning the oldest civilizations.

CHAPTER 9

Early Writing

EARLY WRITING

Some of the pictographs and cuneiform writing that archaeologists have uncovered date to this period. Some researchers have suggested it is possible that Genesis was written on cuneiform tablets and passed from generation to generation until Moses compiled and edited the Genesis we now have.

JUST FOR FUN—MY ATTEMPT TO WRITE CUNEIFORM ON CLAY

Photo by Lois Clymer

3200 BC

ANCIENT HISTORY AT A GLANCE

TRACING THE ANCESTRY OF JESUS CHRIST

Methuselah, at the age of 187, had a son named Lamech (Genesis 5:25).

TIMELINE OF THE FIRST NINE PATRIARCHS

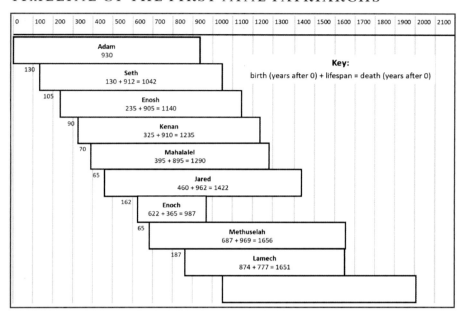

PROFILE OF AN ANCIENT HISTORIAN

Polybius was a Greek historian living around 264–146 BC. His book *The Histories* covered the period he lived in, and specifically, the Punic Wars, in detail. The Punic Wars were fought between the Roman republic and ancient Carthage.

Polybius writes that they were the "longest and most severely contested wars in history." See Chapter 39 for some information on the Punic Wars, including Hannibal's famous attempt to bring elephants over the Alps.

Polybius, iStock.com

CHAPTER 10

Noah, the Tenth Patriarch

TRACING THE ANCESTRY OF JESUS CHRIST

Lamech, at the age of 182 years, had a son named Noah (Genesis 5:28). Noah completes the listing of the first ten patriarchs found in Genesis and the last ten names listed in the genealogy of Jesus Christ.

TIMELINE FOR THE FIRST TEN PATRIARCHS

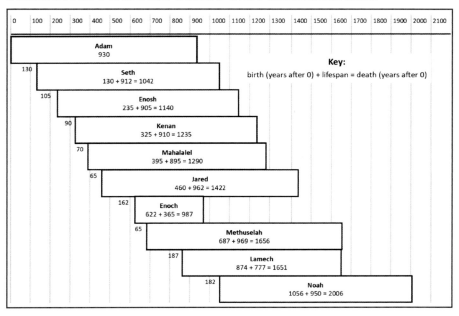

3100 BC

PROFILE OF AN ANCIENT HISTORIAN

Josephus lived AD 37–100. He was a Romano-Jewish historian. He recorded Jewish history with an emphasis on the Jewish-Roman war of the first century AD. He was born into a wealthy Jewish family in Jerusalem, but he defected to the Roman side and was granted Roman citizenship.

CHAPTER 11

Enoch, An Eminent Astronomer

ENOCH, A GODLY MAN

We are told in the Bible that Enoch was a Godly man who did not experience death because God took him. He was also a prophet.

"Enoch walked with God; and he was not, for God took him" (Genesis 5:24).

"By faith Enoch was taken up so that he should not see death" (Hebrews 11:5).

"Enoch, in the seventh generation from Adam, prophesied" (Jude 1:14a).

ARABIAN TRADITION REGARDING ENOCH

An Arabian name for Enoch is Edris. An Arabian tradition for Enoch is that he was an eminent astronomer, mathematician, and prophet of

God.[1] The photo below shows an eclipse. Enoch studied the solar system, so he probably would have identified eclipses.

Photo by Abigail

Drawing of Orion by Layne

---

[1] Edward Hall, *The Wall Chart of World History* (London: Barnes & Noble Publishing, 1988), 4.

CHAPTER 12

The First Astronomers

THE FIRST ASTRONOMERS

According to Josephus, a first-century historian, Seth, and his posterity were the inventors of that "peculiar sort of wisdom which is concerned with the heavenly bodies and their order."[2] They recognized and studied the paths of the sun, the moon, the planets, and the stars. Perhaps, they named the stars and constellations.

THE ZODIAC

Contemporary astronomers tell us that the naming of the constellations is very, very old, and most of the names have been retained through the ages.

---

[2] Flavius Josephus, Book 1 of *The Antiquities of the Jews*, from *The Complete Works of Josephus*, translated by William Whiston (Nashville: Thomas Nelson, 1998), 36.

STARGAZING

Drawing by Layne

THE SUN, MOON, PLANETS, AND STARS

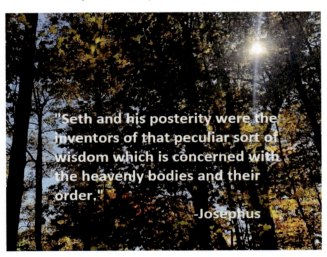

"Seth and his posterity were the inventors of that peculiar sort of wisdom which is concerned with the heavenly bodies and their order."
—Josephus

Photo by Stella

CHAPTER 13

Long Lives of The Patriarchs

LONG LIVES OF THE PATRIARCHS

Adam died at the age of 930, and Seth died at the age of 912. Enosh died at the age of 905 (Genesis 5:3, 6, 9). Because of his long life, Methuselah could have talked with Adam for 243 years. Shem was born 100 years before the Great Flood and lived 500 years after it. He could have talked with Abraham.

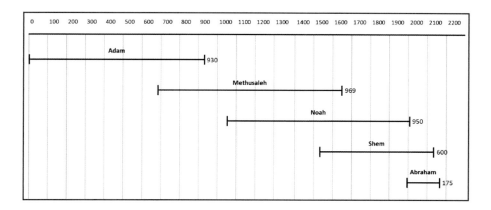

2800 BC

WHO WAS MELCHIZADEK?

The Bible describes a battle of nine kings in Abraham's time and states that Abraham paid tithes and was blessed by Melchizedek, priest, and king of Salem. We wonder who Melchizadek was. It is possible that he was Shem, son of Noah, as he would have still been living. (Noah had already died.) The oldest living father was the king and priest of his tribe.

CHAPTER 14

A Mathematical Decay Curve

LONG LIVES OF THE PATRIARCHS

The rapid decline in human lifespan after the Great Flood seems a remarkable occurrence. What caused it? Nobody knows. Interestingly, the ages fall into a mathematical construct, an exponential decay curve. The lifespans were not a creative invention of some early scribe. This curve can be traced for about forty generations using the birth and death ages given in the Bible. By the time we get to King David, people had what are considered to be normal lifespans.[3]

---

[3] Robert Carter, "The Rapid decline in Biblical lifespans," accessed 12//1/2921 http://creation.com/rapid-decline-biblical-lifespans

EXPONENTIAL DECAY CURVE

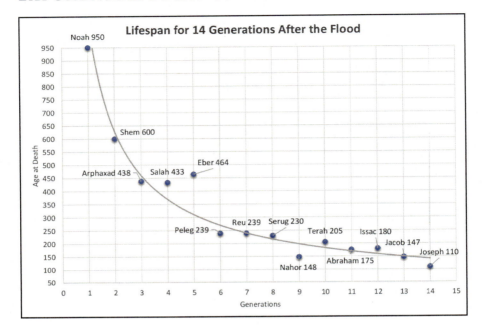

CHAPTER 15

Wickedness of Man Brings Flood

WICKEDNESS OF MAN BRINGS FLOOD

We are told in the Bible that, at this time, "man's wickedness became [great] and every inclination of the thoughts of his heart was only evil all the time. The Lord was grieved that he had made man on the earth, and his heart was filled with pain. So the Lord said, 'I will wipe mankind, whom I have created, from the face of the earth—men and animals, and creatures that move along the ground, and birds of the air—for I am grieved that I have made them.' But Noah found favor in the eyes of the Lord" (Genesis 6:5–8 NIV).

Drawing by Clara

CHAPTER 16

Family of Noah Saved

FAMILY OF NOAH SAVED

Noah was 500 years old when he had a son named Japheth (Genesis 5:32). Around this time, God instructed Noah to make an ark: "Make for yourself an ark of gopher wood; you shall make the ark with rooms and shall cover it inside and out with pitch. This is how you shall make it: the length of the ark, three hundred cubits (about 450 feet), its breadth fifty cubits (about 75 feet), and its height thirty cubits (about 45 feet). You shall make a window for the ark and finish it to a cubit from the top; and set the door of the ark in the side of it; you shall make it with lower, second, and third decks" (Genesis 6:14–16).

2500 BC

Drawing by Clara

EPIC OF GILGAMESH TELLS STORY OF FLOOD

One of the early cuneiform tablets we have found tells of the Great Flood. In the Epic of Gilgamesh, the beginning lines brag that Gilgamesh has knowledge of all things and has handed down things known before the flood. In the epic, Gilgamesh is searching among his ancestors to learn how to regain immortality, which had been lost. He manages to cross the river of death to meet with Uta-Napishtim (Noah), who tells him about the flood. He relates that he was told in a dream to build a boat. He took animals and his family with him, released a dove and a raven, landed on Mount Nisir (which is near Mount Ararat) and sacrificed animals after the flood.

CHAPTER 17

The Promise of the Rainbow

THE GREAT FLOOD

"In the 600th year of Noah's life, on the seventeenth day of the second month, on that day all the springs of the great deep burst open, and the floodgates of the heavens were opened. And rain fell on the earth forty days and forty nights… [The waters] rose greatly on the earth, and all the high mountains under the entire heavens were covered" (Genesis 7:11–12,19 NIV).

SACRIFICE TO GOD AND PROMISE BY GOD

When Noah and his family left the ark, Noah sacrificed to God. God promised he would not send another flood to destroy the whole world and gave the rainbow as a promise.

Photo by Rachel Mohler

2400 BC

CHAPTER 18

Kingdom of Nimrod

KINGDOM OF NIMROD

Cush was the father of Nimrod. "The first centers of his kingdom were Babylon, Erech, Akkad and Calneh in Shinar. From that land he went to Assyria, where he built Nineveh, Rehoboth Ir, Calah, and Resen" (Genesis 10:10–12 NIV).

MAP OF NIMROD'S FIRST CENTERS

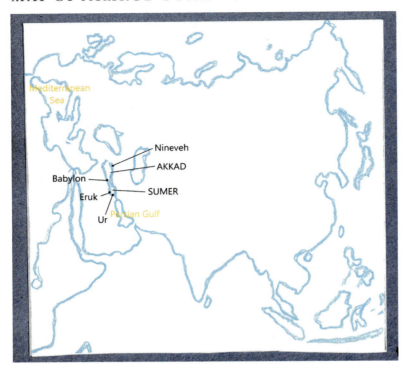

According to Josephus, a historian of the first century AD, Nimrod built Babylon and was the instigator of building the Tower of Babel.[4]

---

[4] Flavius Josephus, Book 1 of *The Antiquities of the Jews*, from *Josephus, The Complete Works*, translated by William Whiston (Nashville: Thomas Nelson, 1998),40.

CHAPTER 19

First Generations after The Great Flood

FIRST GENERATIONS AFTER THE GREAT FLOOD

The first generations after the flood lived to be very old, sometimes outliving their children, grandchildren, and great grandchildren. They were revered, sometimes as gods. People called their land, or, often, their major city, or major river by the name of their founding ancestor (see below).

THE SIXTEEN GRANDSONS OF NOAH

JAPHETH—seven sons:

1. Gomer: Gomerites
2. Magog: Turks
3. Madai: Medes
4. Javan: Jupiter (a god)
5. Tubal: Tobol River

2200 BC

6. Meshech: Moscow
7. Tiras: Thor (a god)

SHEM—five sons

1. Elam: Iran
2. Asshur: Assyrians
3. Arphaxed: Chaldeans
4. Lud: Lydians
5. Aram: Aramaic

HAM—four sons

1. Cush: Cushites
2. Mizraim: Egypt
3. Phut: Phut River
4. Canaan: Canaanites

CHAPTER 20

Egypt and its Pyramids

EGYPT

Constantinus Manasses, a Byzantine chronicler who lived in the twelfth century, wrote that the Egyptian state lasted 1,663 years. Counting backward from the time that Cambyses, King of Persia, conquered Egypt, leads to about this time. Mizraim, son of Ham and grandson of Noah, led his colony into Egypt. *Mizraim* is the Hebrew word for Egypt, which is sometimes called the Land of Mizraim.[5]

THE PYRAMIDS OF EGYPT

Egypt is known for its pyramids. Some sources have counted as many as 118 pyramids. Most of them were built as tombs for Egyptian pharaohs. The most famous pyramids are those at Giza, which is near Cairo. The Pyramid of Khufu is the largest Egyptian pyramid. It is one of the seven wonders of the ancient world. It is the only wonder still standing, and the oldest of the seven wonders.

---

[5] James Ussher, *The Annals of the World*, revised and updated by Larry and Marion Pierce, (Green Forest, AR: MasterBooks, 2003), 22.

PYRAMIDS

Drawing by Lyv

CHAPTER 21

Empire of Sargon

EMPIRE OF SARGON

Sargon came from Akkad (see map below). He was a skilled soldier who built a huge army. He conquered the whole of Sumer and Akkad, possibly creating the world's first empire.

ABRAHAM WAS BORN

Abraham was born around this time. As told in the Bible, he lived in Ur before going to Canaan. He is the father of the Israelites (Jews). It is of Abraham's lineage that Jesus Christ was born. Abraham is the father of three major religions: Judaism, Christianity, and Islam.

ADVANCED CIVILIZATION ALONG THE INDUS VALLEY

An advanced civilization developed in India, along the Indus Valley. Its major cities were Mohenjo-Daro and Harappa. They were carefully planned. In the middle of each city was a walled fortress. Each house was built around an open courtyard and had two or more stories. Houses had bathrooms with a toilet connected to a drain that ran under the street.

MAP OF MESOPOTAMIA AND INDUS VALLEY

CHAPTER 22

The Minoans

THE MINOANS

The people who settled in Crete were called Minoans. They were farmers who kept animals such as sheep and goats and grew wheat and vegetables. They were skilled sailors who built a large fleet of trading vessels, which they sailed all around the Mediterranean. They became successful and wealthy traders. At about this time (1900 BC), they built palaces in each of their towns. The palace at Knossos was the largest, with 1,000 rooms.

The Minoans had a very dangerous sport called bull leaping. Highly trained men grasped the horns of a charging bull and somersaulted over its back. Paintings on the walls of their palaces show this sport.

ABRAHAM LEFT UR

The Bible records the story of Abraham. Abraham left Ur and went to Canaan. He was called by God to become the father of a great nation (the Israelites) through whom Jesus Christ would come someday.

1900 BC

When he was a hundred years old, Abraham had a son, Isaac.

MAP OF CRETE AND ABRAHAM'S UR AND CANAAN

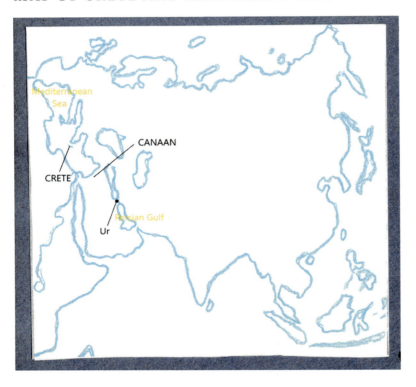

CHAPTER 23

Empire of Hammurabi

HAMMURABI

Around 2000 BC, the lands of Sumer and Akkad were invaded by tribes called Amorites. Around 1800 BC, Hammurabi became king of Babylon. He fought the other Amorite kings and conquered the whole of Sumer and Akkad, creating the first Babylonian Empire. He is famous for his Babylonian Law Code. When he died, the empire fell apart.

1800 BC

MAP OF HAMMURABI EMPIRE

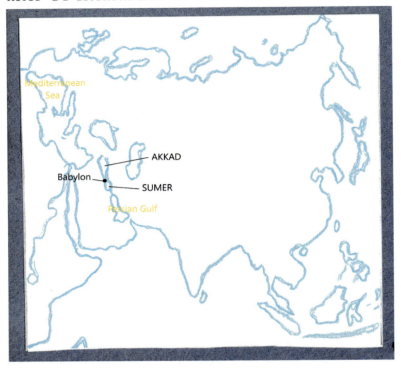

ABRAHAM'S SON AND GRANDSONS

Abraham's son Isaac became the father of two sons, Jacob (later called Israel) and Esau. The two brothers fought over a birthright, and eventually, Jacob moved to get away from Esau. Jacob married Leah and Rachel and had twelve sons, whose descendants became the twelve tribes of the Israelites, as recorded in the Bible.

CHAPTER 24

Family of Jacob (Israel)

THE FAMILY OF JACOB (ISRAEL)

Jacob (later called Israel) had twelve sons, of whom the next to youngest was named Joseph. He was favored by his father and given a coat of many colors. His brothers became jealous of him and sold him into Egypt as a slave. He was a good person and achieved success in the house of the ruler to whom he was sold. Eventually, he became a ruler who saved his people from a famine. The rest of his family joined him in Egypt and settled there. The biblical story of how Joseph met his brothers who had sold him into Egypt is very dramatic. Ultimately, Joseph forgave his brothers.

JOSEPH WITH COAT OF MANY COLORS

Drawing by Cassedy

PEOPLE OF CHINA

The people of China began farming along the banks of the Yellow River. They grew millet, fruits, nuts, and vegetables and kept pigs, dogs, and chickens.

Silkworms make silk thread, which can be spun into fine cloth. The Chinese were the first to discover how to do this.

A large part of China was ruled by the Shang Dynasty from about 1766 BC to 1027 BC.

CHAPTER 25

The Hittite Empire

THE HITTITE PEOPLE

The Hittite people settled in Anatolia (modern Turkey). By this time (1600 BC) they had joined together to form one kingdom, with a capital city at Hattushash. They were tough warriors who invaded Syria and were bitter enemies of the Egyptians.

MAP OF THE HITTITE EMPIRE

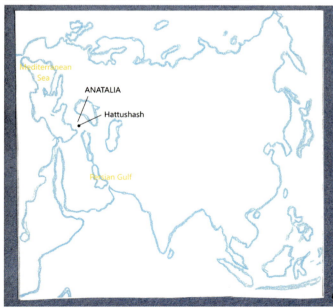

1600 BC

THE WISE MAN JOB

According to Severus Sulpicius, a French chronicler who lived AD 363–425, the wise man Job lived around this time (see the book of Job in the Bible).

Job is the story of a wise and wealthy man who suffered the loss of his family, his possessions, and his health. He had three friends who came to visit him, and they told him he must be evil, or this would not have happened to him. Job maintains his innocence and questions why this has happened to him. God speaks to him in a whirlwind, saying in effect, who are you to understand God? Job replies, Surely, I spoke of things I did not understand. "Therefore I retract, and I repent in dust and ashes" (Job 42:6).

CHAPTER 26

Moses Leads Israelites Out of Egypt

MOSES SAVES THE ISRAELITES FROM BONDAGE

When the Israelites were living in Egypt, the pharaoh felt threatened by them. So, he made them slaves and mistreated them. Moses was born to Amram and Jochebed, who was the daughter of Levi, the son of Jacob. The Israelites were being told to throw all their baby boys into the Nile River. Moses' mother put him into a basket, which she hid in the river among the reeds. It was found by the pharaoh's daughter, who raised Moses as her son. This story is found in the Bible.

When Moses became an adult, he led the Israelites in their escape from Egypt. They eventually settled in Canaan.

1500 BC

EGYPT IS KNOWN FOR ITS PYRAMIDS

Drawing by Clara

TUTHMOSIS II

The Egyptian empire was at its greatest around 1500 BC. Tuthmosis II was a great warrior pharaoh who led his army to war seventeen times, battling enemies who included the Hittites.

CHAPTER 27

The Mycenae People

THE MYCENAE PEOPLE (GREEKS)

The country now known as Greece was divided into small kingdoms, each made up of a walled city and the land around it. The most important kingdom was Mycenae. So, the people of Greece became known as Mycenaeans.

MYCENAEAN WARRIORS TOOK CONTROL OF CRETE

In 1450 BC, Mycenaean warriors took control of Crete, destroying palaces in the process. The Minoan civilization gradually died out and was replaced by the Mycenaean civilization.

THE GREEKS AT WAR

War was an important part of Mycenaean life. All the city-states had their own army and they were often at war with each other. Kings and nobles were trained as warriors and skilled metal workers made weapons from bronze. The bravery of soldiers was idealized in poems.

1400 BC

MAP OF GREECE AND CRETE

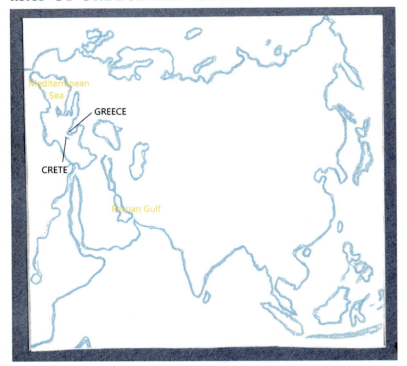

CHAPTER 28

City of Troy Destroyed

CITY OF TROY DESTROYED BY MYCENAEANS

Around 1250 BC, the city of Troy (in modern Turkey) was destroyed by the Mycenaeans (Greeks). There is a famous tale about this real event. How much truth is in the tale we do not know.

The Trojan horse was a huge, hollow, wooden horse built by the Greeks to trick the people of Troy during the war between the Trojans and the Greeks. The Greeks pretended to desert the war. They sailed away, leaving behind a man who persuaded the Trojans that the horse was an offering to the goddess Athena, who would make it impossible for Greek soldiers to enter the city.

TROJAN HORSE
Drawing by Amelia

1300 BC

Despite warnings, the horse was taken inside the city gates. During the night, Greek soldiers emerged from the Trojan horse and opened the gates of the city to allow in the Greek army, which had returned.

CHAPTER 29

The Phoenicians

The Phoenicians lived at the eastern end of the Mediterranean Sea and may have descended from the Canaanites. They became very successful traders. The main trading posts were the cities of Tyre, Sidon, and Bylos. The Phoenicians were famous for their purple dye. Their name comes from a Greek word that means "purple men."

They were excellent sailors, who sailed all over the Mediterranean, and even went as far as the British Isles.

SAILBOAT

Drawing by Clara

1200 BC

Trading posts were established all around the Mediterranean. A famous trading post was Carthage, on the north coast of Africa. The Phoenicians were greatly valued for their successful trading. In time, they became part of the great empires of Assyria, Babylon, Persia, and Alexander the Great.

MAP OF CITIES OF PHOENICIA AND THE CITY OF CARTHAGE

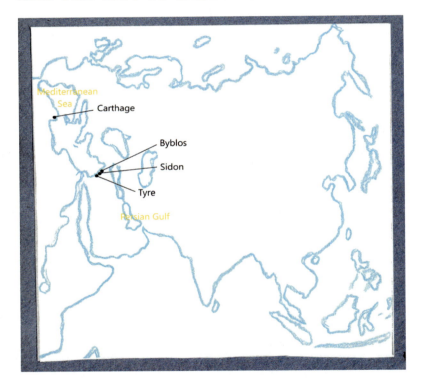

CHAPTER 30

The Israelites

THE ISRAELITES

The Bible tells the history of the Israelites. The Israelites (the twelves sons of Jacob) became slaves in Egypt and were led by Moses to freedom in Canaan. They gained land in Canaan and built cities and towns. Goats and sheep were kept for meat and milk. They grew olive trees and fig trees and made wine from their grape vines. Their gardens produced beans, garlic, onions, and lentils.

ISRAELITE BOY WITH SHEEP

Drawing by Layne

1100 BC

KINGS OF ISRAEL

Saul became the first king of Israel and David became the second king. They fought and defeated the Philistines in many battles. David's son Solomon was the next king.

Crown by Amelia

THE SEA PEOPLES

An army of sea peoples destroyed the Hittite empire and then attacked Egypt but were defeated. They were scattered around the Mediterranean. One tribe, called the Peleset (also known as the Philistines), settled in southern Canaan, which was later named Palestine, after them. Many stories of the Hittites and the Philistines are recorded in the Bible.

CHAPTER 31

King Solomon of Israel

ISRAEL BECAME POWERFUL DURING KING SOLOMON'S REIGN

King Solomon, son of King David (965–928 BC, according to Usborne[6]), built a beautiful temple, filled with gold, bronze, and precious metals. The walls were covered with gold. Phoenician craftsmen helped to build the temple.

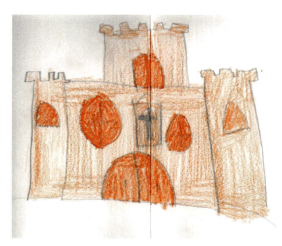

Drawing by Lyv

---

[6] Jane Bingham, Fiona Chandler, and Sam Taplin, *The Usborne Internet-Linked Encyclopedia of World History* (London: Usborne Publishing, 2000), 143.

1000 BC

King Solomon traded with other countries and became rich and powerful. The kingdom of Israel, during this time, was established in Canaan on the east coast of the Mediterranean.

Along the south coast of Arabia, kingdoms grew up. The most famous was Sabaea (Sheba). Merchants from India and China brought spices, silk, and jewels to ports on the southern coast of Arabia. Sabaea became wealthy as an important post on the trade routes. In the Bible, we read about the Queen of Sheba visiting King Solomon.

ZHOU DYNASTY BEGINS IN CHINA

Around this time, the Shang Dynasty in China was conquered by people called the Zhou. The Zhou dynasty lasted until 221 BC, when Qin Shi Huangdi became China's first emperor.

CHAPTER 32

The Celts

THE CELTS

There were many different Celtic tribes, but they all shared a similar way of life and language. They spread out across Europe, setting up farms and small villages. Their houses were built of wood or stones, with a thatched roof and one spacious room, where the family cooked, ate, and slept.

A CELTIC HOUSE
Drawing by Clara

900 BC

The Celts were fierce warriors, and they built forts on hilltops to protect their women and animals. As the Roman empire grew, the Celts fought hard to defend their lands. In 390 BC, the Celts destroyed part of Rome. Eventually, most of the Celts were conquered.

CHAPTER 33

Fall of Israel

FALL OF ISRAEL

We read the story of the Israelites in the Old Testament of the Bible. The Israelites were the people from whom Jesus Christ was descended.

After King Solomon died, the Israelite nation was split into two kingdoms. Israel was in the north and Judah in the south. Later, the people of Judah were called Jews. In the Bible, we read that both kingdoms failed to follow the commandments of God. They pursued the gods and the evil practices of the peoples living around them. Prophets warned the people that unless they returned to God, they would be conquered and suffer much.

You can read about the fall of Israel and Judah in the Bible just as you can read it in modern history books drawn from a variety of sources. Below is a timeline taken from the *Usborne Encyclopedia of World History*.

800 BC

CAPTURE OF ISRAEL AND JUDAH BY ASSYRIA AND BABYLON[7]

> **Assyria and Babylon capture Israel and Judah**
>
> 1000 BC Assyria becomes powerful
>
> 730 BC Assyria takes control of Babylon
>
> 722 BC Assyria invades Israel and takes captives
>
> 612 BC Babylon and the Medes defeat Assyria
>
> 605 BC Babylon is rebuilt by Nebuchadnezzar
>
> 587 BC Babylon destroys Jerusalem and takes captives
>
> 539 BC Persia captures Babylon
>
> *Dates are from Usborne Encyclopedia of World History*

---

[7] Jane Bingham, Fiona Chandler, and Sam Taplin, *The Usborne Internet-Linked Encyclopedia of World History* (London: Usborne Publishing, 2000), 143, 149, 151.

CHAPTER 34

Assyrian Empire

HISTORY OF EMPIRES

Two empires grew strong in the Mesopotamian region: the Assyrian and the Babylonian Empires. They competed fiercely. Then a third empire from the southeast (Persia) overtook them.

The Assyrian Empire was strong from 1000–663 BC. King Ashurnasipal II built Nimrud and King Sennacherib built Nineveh. He destroyed the city of Babylon in 689 BC. Sennacherib expanded the city of Nineveh and built great city walls, many temples, and a royal garden. He is famous for his Southwest Palace which he called "Palace without Rival." Stories of King Sennacherib are found in the Bible. King Ashurnasipal is also mentioned in the Bible.

The empire collapsed when attacked by the Medes and Babylonians around 612 BC.

700 BC

MAP OF THE ASSYRIAN EMPIRE

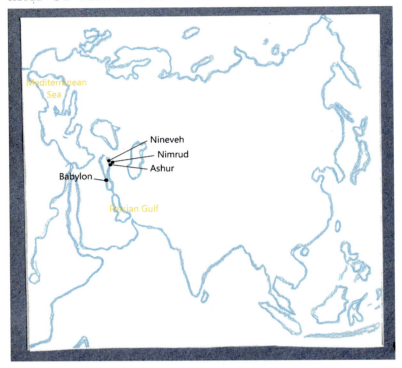

CHAPTER 35

Babylonian Empire

THE BABYLONIAN EMPIRE

Babylon had been destroyed by the Assyrians, but when Assyria was defeated in 625 BC, Babylon was rebuilt by King Napbopolassar and his son King Nebuchadnezzar II. King Nebuchadnezzar built the Hanging Gardens of Babylon, one of the seven wonders of the ancient world. Stories of King Nebuchadnezzar are found in the Bible.

MAP OF BABYLONIAN EMPIRE

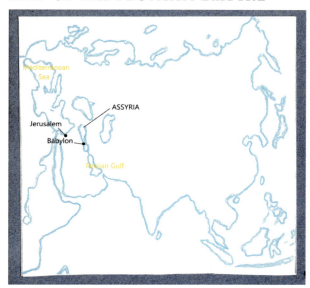

600 BC

Daniel, of the Bible, was captured by the Babylonians around this time and taken to Babylonia.

CHINESE PHILOSOPHER AND POLITICIAN CONFUCIUS

Confucius was born in 551 BC. He was a philosopher and politician and considered a great Chinese sage. His teaching and philosophy remain popular in China today.

SIDDHARTHA GAUTAMA, BUDDHA

Siddhartha Gautama (Buddha) lived around 560–480 BC in India. He is regarded as the founder of Buddhism and revered for his enlightenment.

CHAPTER 36

Persian Empire

THE PERSIAN EMPIRE

Persia was an ancient kingdom in today's Iran. In early times it had been invaded by two tribes—the Medes from the North and the Persians from the South. The Medes and Persians are mentioned in the Bible.

Around 550 BC, the Persian King Cyrus II defeated the Medes and took over their lands. He went on to build a large empire that became the largest empire the world had yet seen. King Cyrus is mentioned many times in the Bible. Under his reign, the Jews were permitted to return to Israel after seventy years of captivity in Babylon.

In 539 BC the Persian Empire overtook Babylon and Babylon became part of the Persian Empire.

Drawing by Lyv

500 BC

KING DARIUS

King Darius of the Persian Empire became very wealthy. He built a magnificent palace at Persepolis. He collected taxes from the people living all across his empire, but he allowed these people to keep their religion and their way of life.

MAP OF PERSIAN EMPIRE

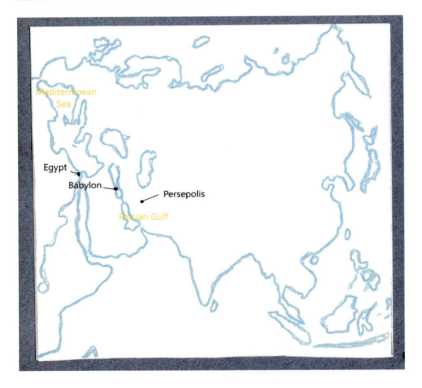

CHAPTER 37

Persians Attack Greece

THE PERSIANS ATTACK GREECE

In 490 BC, the Persians invaded Greece. The Greeks fought back and defeated them in a battle at a place called Marathon. A runner carried the good news approximately twenty-six miles to Athens, where he died of exhaustion. The modern marathon races are named after this event.

In 480 BC, the Persians attacked Greece again. This time they built a bridge by tying a group of boats together with ropes, and the Persian soldiers walked across the bridge at a place known as Hellespont. They marched into Greece and destroyed the city of Athens.

400 BC

CROSSING AT HELLESPONT

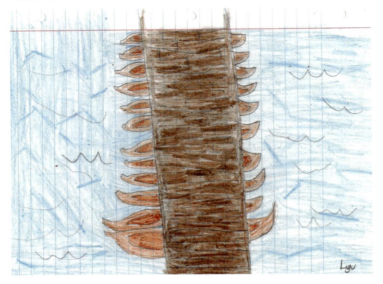

Drawing by Lyv

SOCRATES AND PLATO

Socrates and Plato were famous philosopher-teachers who lived in Athens, where democracy began.

CHAPTER 38

Alexander the Great

ALEXANDER THE GREAT

The Macedonian King Philip II, who lived north of Greece, built up a strong army with which he began to conquer the Greek city states. By 338 BC, he controlled all of Greece. When he was murdered, his twenty-year-old son, Alexander, became king. Alexander was a brilliant commander who created the largest empire yet known. He conquered Egypt and Phoenicia.

ALEXANDER THE GREAT
Drawing by Cassedy

300 BC

He built cities all over his empire and named them after himself—for example, the city of Alexandria in Egypt.

Alexander tried to reach India but failed, and on his return, he caught a fever and died in Babylon at the age of thirty-three.

After his death, his empire broke up as his generals fought each other for control.

CHAPTER 39

The Punic Wars

THE PUNIC WARS

Around this time there was a series of wars between Rome and Carthage known as the Punic Wars. Each side fought over who should control trade around the Mediterranean. Hannibal of Carthage is famous for bringing elephants over the Alps. The wars ended in 146 BC, when Carthage was destroyed by the Romans, who went on to conquer kingdoms around the Mediterranean.

ZHOU DYNASTY ENDS

In 221 BC, the Zhou dynasty ended, and Qin Shi Huangdi became emperor. He controlled a huge empire and built some sections of the Great Wall of China. He died in 210 BC and was buried with a terracotta army.

In 202 BC, the Han dynasty began. The Han ruled for the next 400 years.

200 BC

GREAT WALL OF CHINA

Drawing by Lyv

CHAPTER 40

The Roman Empire

THE ROMAN EMPIRE

Until 500 BC, Rome was ruled by kings. When the last king was driven out, Rome became a republic. Led by the Senate, Rome gradually conquered all of Italy.

In 49 BC, the Roman general Julius Caesar seized power. He was stabbed to death by senators, and a series of power struggles followed. In 31 BC, Augustus became the first emperor of Rome. Over the next 150 years, the Romans conquered more land. Their empire eventually stretched from Britain to the Middle East.

JESUS CHRIST WAS BORN

Jesus Christ was born around 4 BC. The New Testament of the Bible tells of his life and ministry, his miracles, his death on the cross and his resurrection.

100 BC

THE CROSS AND THE EMPTY TOMB

This drawing shows the empty tomb of Jesus Christ after his crucifixion and resurrection from the dead. You can see the stone rolled away and the crosses in the background. You can also see Jesus Christ's burial garment, which he left behind when he was resurrected. It has a faint image on it, a miracle we can see today (Shroud of Turin). Because of Jesus Christ, we can also have life after death if we believe in him. "I am the resurrection and the life; he who believes in Me will live even if he dies" (John 11:25).

Drawing by Clara

About the Author

Photo by Stella

Made in the USA
Middletown, DE
24 May 2022